INSIDE
DIVERGENT

Printed and bound in Italy by L.E.G.O Spa, Italy.

ISBN 978-0-00-755538-3

Book design by Victor Joseph Ochoa
14 15 16 17 18   LP/RRDC   10 9 8 7 6 5 4 3 2 1
❖
First Edition

MIX
Paper from
responsible sources
FSC   FSC C007454
www.fsc.org

FSC™ is a non-profit international organisation established to promote
the responsible management of the world's forests. Products carrying the
FSC label are independently certified to assure consumers that they come
from forests that are managed to meet the social, economic and ecological
needs of present and future generations, and other controlled sources.

Find out more about HarperCollins and the environment at
www.harpercollins.co.uk/green

CONTENTS

4   Introduction

12   The Five Factions

48   The Initiates

64   The Faction Members

82   The Choice

106   Becoming Dauntless

INTRODUCTION

THIS IS THE CHICAGO OF THE FUTURE

The once-great city and its land-marks—the Sears Tower, the Ferris wheel at Navy Pier, the El trains, and the Hancock building—have fallen into disrepair. What was formerly Lake Michigan is now a barren marshland. A fence wraps around the entire city, guarding its citizens.

But despite outward appearances, this futuristic city has emerged as something that the old Chicago never was: It is a utopia, a perfect society, a place free of conflict.

Unless, of course, you are discovered to be . . .

DIVER

WHAT IS A DIVERGENT?

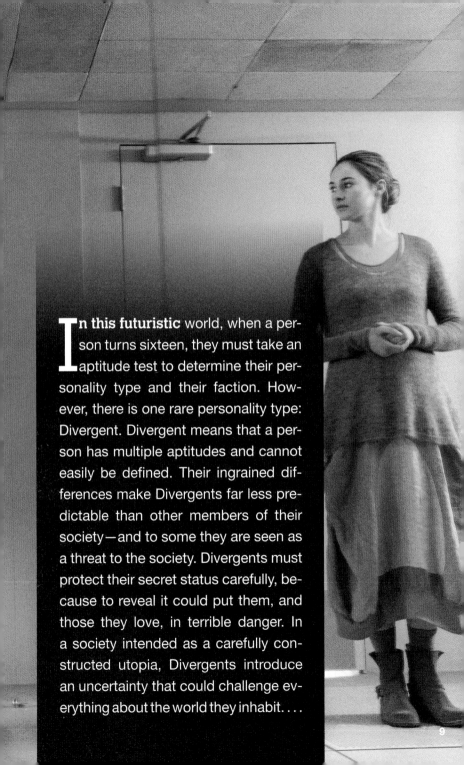

In this futuristic world, when a person turns sixteen, they must take an aptitude test to determine their personality type and their faction. However, there is one rare personality type: Divergent. Divergent means that a person has multiple aptitudes and cannot easily be defined. Their ingrained differences make Divergents far less predictable than other members of their society—and to some they are seen as a threat to the society. Divergents must protect their secret status carefully, because to reveal it could put them, and those they love, in terrible danger. In a society intended as a carefully constructed utopia, Divergents introduce an uncertainty that could challenge everything about the world they inhabit. . . .

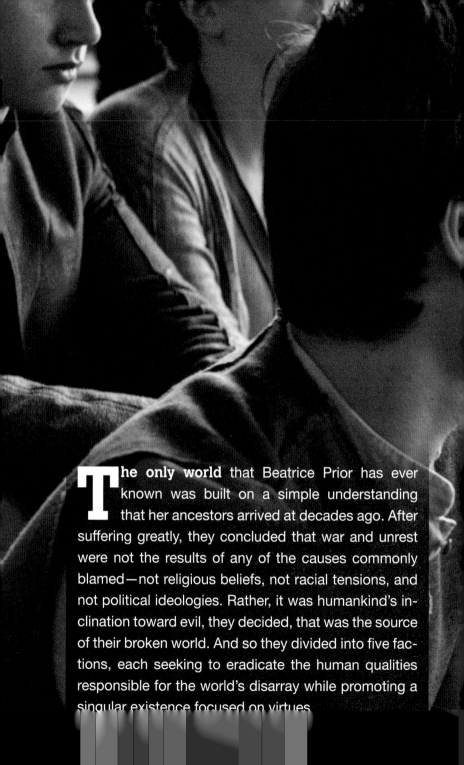

The **only world** that Beatrice Prior has ever known was built on a simple understanding that her ancestors arrived at decades ago. After suffering greatly, they concluded that war and unrest were not the results of any of the causes commonly blamed—not religious beliefs, not racial tensions, and not political ideologies. Rather, it was humankind's inclination toward evil, they decided, that was the source of their broken world. And so they divided into five factions, each seeking to eradicate the human qualities responsible for the world's disarray while promoting a singular existence focused on virtues.

ABNEGATION
The Selfless

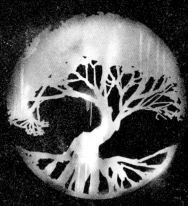

AMITY
The Peaceful

CANDOR
The Honest

ERUDITE
The Intelligent

DAUNTLESS
The Brave

THE FIVE FACTIONS

ABNEGATION
The Selfless

I WILL FORGET THE ONES I LOVE IF I DO NOT SERVE THEM.

—From the Abnegation Faction Manifesto

Abnegation

believes that selfishness is the root of evil. This faction embraces selflessness and rejects intellectual curiosity, personal reflection, and creativity—finding these behaviors self-centered and individualistic. Modest and self-effacing, they work to improve the collective, public good.

A bnegation members eschew both collective and personal thoughts of identity. Instead, they focus on the constant service of others, whose needs must always be valued above the self and its desires.

Family plays a key role in the daily life of this faction. The Abnegation neighborhood resembles military-style housing. Simple houses are identical to one another in size, design, and structure. All are painted in the same neutral tone, and personalization of the exterior is strictly prohibited. Inside, homes are configured simply yet effectively, to serve the needs of the family unit, so that they, in turn, can best serve others. Family members show their love for one another through daily acts of service and self-sacrifice.

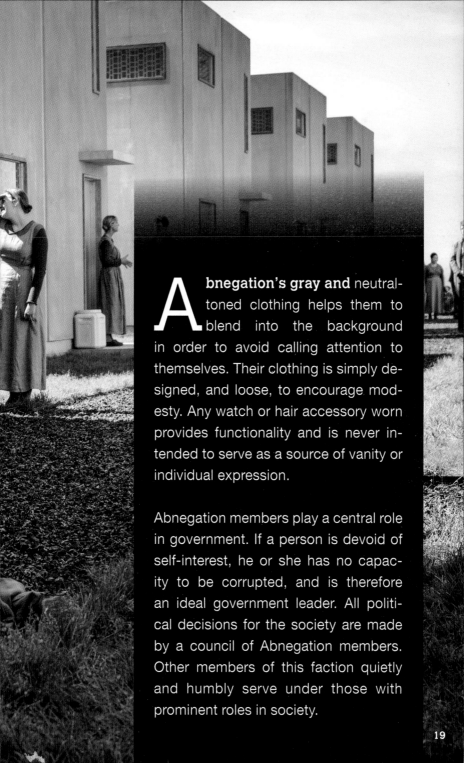

Abnegation's gray and neutral-toned clothing helps them to blend into the background in order to avoid calling attention to themselves. Their clothing is simply designed, and loose, to encourage modesty. Any watch or hair accessory worn provides functionality and is never intended to serve as a source of vanity or individual expression.

Abnegation members play a central role in government. If a person is devoid of self-interest, he or she has no capacity to be corrupted, and is therefore an ideal government leader. All political decisions for the society are made by a council of Abnegation members. Other members of this faction quietly and humbly serve under those with prominent roles in society.

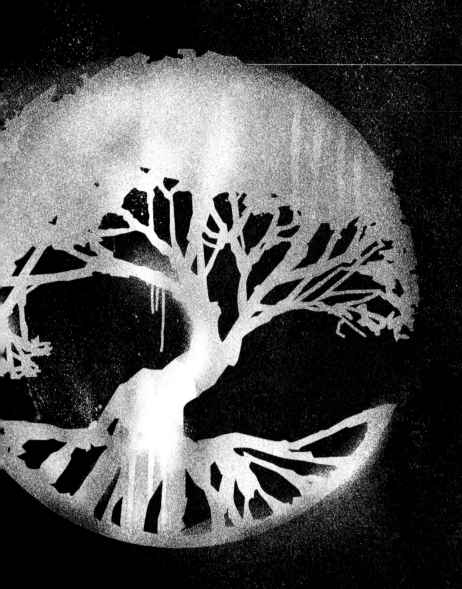

AMITY
The Peaceful

CRUEL THOUGHTS LEAD TO CRUEL WORDS, AND HURT YOU AS MUCH AS THEY HURT THEIR TARGET.

—From the Amity Faction Manifesto

Amity

values peacefulness and harmony above all and believes that aggression is the source of all discord. Free-spirited, trusting, and often artistic, they believe in conflict resolution through peaceful dialogue.

Amity members celebrate the joys and gifts of nature, since a meaningful relationship with nature is closely linked to inner peace. They place a high value on creativity and the beauty that artistic persons can bring to the world. Competitiveness, worry, judgment, and feelings of inadequacy are foreign concepts to the Amity faction.

Communal living is at the heart of Amity life. Members live together and share meals in large groups where family relationships and friendships are valued equally. Amity's work is chiefly devoted to food production for the entire city, so daily life means vigorous labor—in the fashion of a traditional farming community—and joyful celebration after work is done.

Amity members **dress** in red and yellow, the two colors they associate with joy. All styles of clothing are acceptable as long as shades of the faction colors are represented. Other aspects of appearance—hairstyles, accessories, and personal grooming—are up to individuals, the point being to express their personalities in ways that bring them joy.

Amity is one of the most essential factions because its farms, greenhouses, and other resources are responsible for the entire city's food production and water purification. A minor segment of the Amity serves the other factions as mediators, counselors, and caretakers. Amity also produces a high proportion of the society's artists, musicians, and writers.

CANDOR
The Honest

LIKE A WILD ANIMAL, THE TRUTH IS TOO POWERFUL TO REMAIN CAGED. WE WILL RAISE OUR CHILDREN TO TELL THE TRUTH.

—From the Candor Faction Manifesto

Candor

believes in honesty and authenticity, at all costs. Lying, secret keeping, and dishonesty are seen as the direct cause of conflict in relationships and in communities. The people of Candor believe that truth makes them inextricable from one another, or impossible to separate. Truth is the "glue" that holds this faction together.

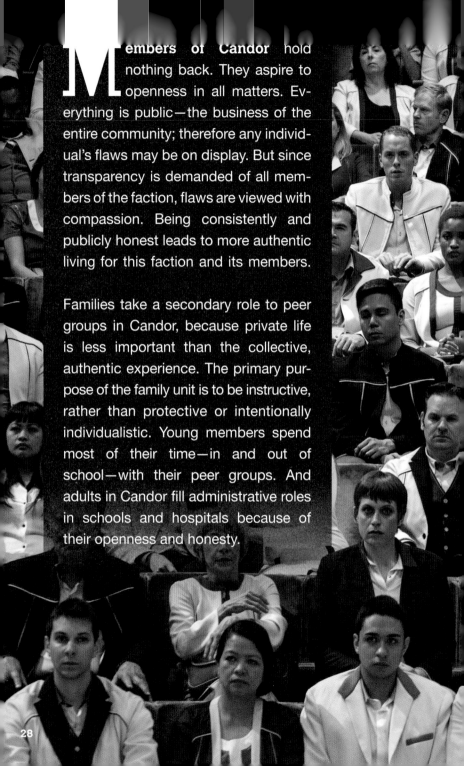

Members of Candor hold nothing back. They aspire to openness in all matters. Everything is public—the business of the entire community; therefore any individual's flaws may be on display. But since transparency is demanded of all members of the faction, flaws are viewed with compassion. Being consistently and publicly honest leads to more authentic living for this faction and its members.

Families take a secondary role to peer groups in Candor, because private life is less important than the collective, authentic experience. The primary purpose of the family unit is to be instructive, rather than protective or intentionally individualistic. Young members spend most of their time—in and out of school—with their peer groups. And adults in Candor fill administrative roles in schools and hospitals because of their openness and honesty.

Truth and dishonesty are seen as black and white, so the members of Candor wear only those two colors—both in every outfit. In terms of personal style, Candor are not as conservative as Abnegation, but they are not as bold as Dauntless, or as carefree as Amity—rather, they are similar to Erudite.

Candor's role in society is to uphold the laws of the individual factions—and of the society as a whole. Members of Candor serve as judges, lawyers, religious leaders, and reporters. They play key roles in working with other factions as well, where they advise on matters of fairness, justice, and leadership.

DAUNTLESS

The Brave

WE BELIEVE
IN FREEDOM FROM FEAR,
IN DENYING FEAR
THE POWER TO INFLUENCE
OUR DECISIONS.

WE DO NOT BELIEVE
IN LIVING COMFORTABLE
LIVES.

—From the Dauntless Faction Manifesto

Courage

is the virtue of the Dauntless faction. For the Dauntless, a commitment to bravery is more critical than anything— than peace, the opinions of others, or even safety. Various Dauntless would define "courage" differently. Some perceive it as fearlessness, striving to eradicate fear in all forms from their lives. Others view it as the boldness that conjures up action in the face of fear. No matter which definition of courage they espouse, all Dauntless thrive on the freedom that comes with bravery.

The Dauntless are the guardians and protectors of the city and the society. Their strength and power comes both from personal behaviors and from the collective heroics of their faction. Other factions may perceive the Dauntless as loud, rowdy, reckless, or overly fixated on tattoos and body piercings, but even these detractors would admit that the Dauntless have an exceptional vitality and zeal for life.

In the Dauntless compound, feats of bravery are as important to the individuals performing them as they are to the members observing and taking inspiration from them. There is an emphasis on physicality, defense, and technology in most every aspect of Dauntless daily life. Diversity reigns in Dauntless, and a family unit can take on a wide variety of appearances and structures, some including both blood relatives and friends.

The **Dauntless dress** in tight-fitting black clothing, which aids in their very physical lifestyle. Radical clothing styles are common, as are bold hair colors and styles. Tattoos, piercings, and body modifications are so common that there is a tattoo shop in the compound.

Security is the chief role performed by Dauntless. Many guard the streets of the city or the perimeter of the fence, while others do surveillance monitoring. Dauntless members take pride in the independence of their faction. Many of them perform roles within the compound—as cooks, nurses, tattoo artists, and trainers—that increase the self-reliance of the faction.

ERUDITE
The Intelligent

INTELLIGENCE IS A GIFT, NOT A RIGHT. IT MUST BE WIELDED NOT AS A WEAPON BUT AS A TOOL FOR THE BETTERMENT OF OTHERS.

—From the Erudite Faction Manifesto

Erudite

places the highest value not only on intelligence but also on knowledge, understanding, innovation, and curiosity. They focus on putting their knowledge to use, in order to develop and discover newer and more advanced sources of information. Their hunger to learn is matched by an equal desire to share knowledge with others.

Like a university campus, the Erudite compound houses libraries, classrooms, and laboratories. Erudite families center around providing educational life lessons and teaching logic and reasoning skills to their children. As children approach adolescence and narrow their fields of study, apprentice-like mentor/mentee relationships often become as or more important than family bonds.

The **Erudite dress** in blue because it is scientifically proven to produce a sense of calm, and calm minds are more readily able to absorb knowledge and find clarity. Members of Erudite maintain a well-groomed and clean-cut appearance, and place little emphasis on personal style.

Erudite's function in society is essential. Its members—the educators, scholars, researchers, technology developers, scientists of various disciplines, and medical workers—are considered critical to a growing and productive society. Erudite works with Amity to make food production more efficient, and with Dauntless to develop technology for security, surveillance, and simulation.

The factionless

The **factionless are** not a true faction. The description is given to those who fail to complete initiation into their chosen faction, or who leave a faction for any reason. They do not have a manifesto, a symbol, or any collective or unifying principles, because they are discouraged from taking on faction-like behaviors.

Faction members pity the factionless, because they must live without the support and community at the heart of the faction-based system. The government offers "useful" work to the factionless, giving them responsibilities such as train and bus operation, delivery work, and serving on janitorial, maintenance, and construction crews. The hope of the society's authorities is that meaningful, regular work will not only provide for the basic needs of the factionless but also instill some of the purpose and intention that the factionless lose by living without a sense of identity or belonging.

The factionless wear ragged clothes discarded or donated by other factions. There is no significance to the odd combinations of faction colors that they wear, and no attention given to personal style. When they are not working the jobs they've been assigned by the government, it is assumed, though not authorized, that they gather in de facto camps to share resources. These factionless groups are based on proximity and basic necessity, rather than being united by choice, virtue, or intention. Abnegation do-gooders often concern themselves with improving the quality of life for the factionless, but members of other factions largely ignore their existence.

THE *INITIATES*

Faction of Origin: Abnegation

 Chosen Faction: Dauntless

"THE TEST WAS SUPPOSED TO TELL ME WHAT FACTION TO CHOOSE."

The rules and dictates of the Abnegation faction are all Tris has ever known, but they still don't come naturally to her. Secretly, she covets the chance to become something more than selfless. But she also deeply loves her family, and the idea of permanently leaving them tears at her heart. With conflicting desires weighing upon her, Choosing Day is already of monumental importance for Beatrice—and then she learns a secret about herself that both explains, and changes, everything.

CALEB PRIOR

 Faction of Origin: Abnegation

 Chosen Faction: Erudite

"YOU HAVE TO THINK OF THE FAMILY... BUT YOU ALSO HAVE TO THINK OF YOURSELF."

Caleb is endlessly thoughtful, humble, helpful, and observant of others, and he genuinely seems happiest when he is putting someone else's needs above his own. But there is a silent curiosity brewing under his calm demeanor. And though his decision to join Erudite shocks his family, and his entire faction of origin, Caleb is decisive. Once he has made his choice, he does not look back.

PETER

 Faction of Origin: Candor

 Chosen Faction: Dauntless

"YOU LOOK LIKE YOU'RE ABOUT TO CRY. I MIGHT GO EASY ON YOU IF YOU CRY."

Raised with Candor's tendency toward brutal honesty, Peter also developed a physical brutality, and a mercilessly cruel personality streak. Throughout Dauntless initiation, he torments the other initiates physically and emotionally: mocking their fears, belittling their weaknesses, and attacking at moments when they are unprotected. Like most tyrants, Peter has built alliances with a few similarly intense peers, but it's clear that he'll think little of ultimately betraying these so-called friends if necessary.

CHRISTINA

 Faction of Origin: Candor

 Chosen Faction: Dauntless

"YOU THINK THIS IS HARD, TRY TELLING THE TRUTH ALL THE TIME..."

Christina never tells less than the truth, even if it means accidentally insulting her peers or disrespecting authority. Bold and brash by nature, but craving privacy, Christina chose a life devoted to external action, rather than the constant, critical self-analysis demanded of her original faction. Perhaps opposite upbringings attract, because she and Tris rapidly develop a close bond amidst the crazy pressures of Dauntless initiation.

WILL

 Faction of Origin: Erudite

 Chosen Faction: Dauntless

"SEE? THE STATS DON'T LIE."

Will knows bits of information about every topic imaginable and is never shy about offering them or about launching into scholarly explanations that interest no one. He's jovial and good-natured, though as willing as anyone to poke fun at his own over-intelligent tendencies. This vivacious warmth, unlike the coldly factual nature of most Erudite, led him to Dauntless. Like Tris, while Will loved some things about his former life, he yearned for something more, beyond the faction he'd always known.

MOLLY

 Faction of Origin: Candor

 Chosen Faction: Dauntless

"HOW LONG DO WE FIGHT FOR?"

Molly lacks the wicked charisma of her ally Peter and is more of a follower than a leader, but like him, an unpleasant mean streak and an intimidating physicality are Molly's primary personality traits. To the other initiates, Molly is daunting: She is unfriendly and she fights dirty. Tanklike in a fight, she rejoices in easily defeating her competitors in sparring matches, making her a favorite of the also-brutal Dauntless coach, Eric.

Faction of Origin: Amity

 Chosen Faction: Dauntless

> *"I JUST HATE EVERYONE WHO'S BETTER THAN ME."*

Al might look like he can handle anything, but as a former Amity, he seems far too good-hearted and gentle to survive Dauntless initiation, and his friends Tris, Christina, and Will fear for his vulnerabilities. Al especially admires Tris and her growing strength, but she only pities his weaknesses. Al chose Dauntless because he liked the idea of a life devoted to protecting others, but he doesn't even seem quite able to protect himself in Dauntless. Instead, he appears to accept the fact that he might fail initiation and become factionless.

THE FACTION MEMBERS

Faction: Dauntless

Dauntless Control Room Operator and Instructor of Non-Dauntless-Born Initiates

"EVERYONE'S AFRAID
OF SOMETHING.
I IGNORE IT...."

Intentionally private about most matters, Tobias believes that fearlessness means dominating personal weaknesses and learning from the courage of others, instead of using brutality to counteract fear. When he isn't training initiates, he works in the Dauntless control room, and though he respects many, it is rare for him to form personal connections. Admired by his fellow faction members but openly disliked by a few of its leaders for his power and charisma, Tobias has a strong sense of self, an intelligent sense of humor, a watchful, protective nature, and a well-defined moral code.

ANDREW PRIOR

Faction: Abnegation

Member of the Governing Council

"IT'S ESSENTIAL THAT WE STICK TOGETHER AS A FACTION—AND AS A FAMILY."

As a respected Abnegation member, Andrew humbly serves on the Governing Council, monitoring the harmony of the entire city. As father to Caleb and Beatrice, and husband to Natalie, Andrew attempts to imbue his family members with the political beliefs and faction priorities that have shaped his life. A man of deep integrity and honor, Andrew is disheartened by the choices that his children make at the Choosing Ceremony. To him, these are betrayals of the greatest magnitude.

NATALIE PRIOR

Faction: Abnegation

Councilman's Wife

"I LOVE YOU... NO MATTER WHAT."

As the spouse of a councilman, Natalie upholds the Abnegation lifestyle, devoting significant energies to serving those most in need, such as the factionless. But there is also a quiet strength and independence of spirit to Natalie. Unlike her husband, she seems supportive, almost encouraging, of Beatrice and Caleb's faction transfers, as if maybe she knew all along who her children would become. And gradually, Tris comes to see that there was perhaps far more depth to her mother than the Abnegation lifestyle showed.

MARCUS EATON

Faction: Abnegation

Leader of the Governing Council

"FACTION BEFORE BLOOD."

Marcus and Andrew have a deep mutual respect for each other after years of working closely. Recently, however, disturbing reports have spread through the city about Marcus. They accuse him of being an abusive father and husband, and question whether he is a fit leader. Marcus and his supporters insist that the rumors are negative propaganda created by the Erudite faction in its campaign to upset the city's balance of power and take a more prominent role in the society's leadership.

Faction: Erudite

Erudite Faction Leader

"I WANT YOU TO CHOOSE WHO YOU TRULY ARE AND WHERE YOU TRULY BELONG—"

Cold and precise, sharp and demanding, Erudite faction leader Jeanine Matthews embodies the chilly professionalism and hyper-intelligence of her faction. Jeanine is willing to employ any tactic necessary to achieve her agenda—whether seeding and spreading lies, backstabbing, building unethical alliances, betraying, torturing, or even indirectly murdering. Because of her brilliant machinations and sly ability to use people's weaknesses to serve her needs, few recognize the full, terrible potential of Jeanine Matthews.

TORI WU

Faction: Dauntless

Tattoo Artist and Aptitude Test Administrator

"IF YOU DON'T FIT INTO A CATEGORY, THEY CAN'T CONTROL YOU."

Born into Erudite, Tori is now a fierce, wise member of Dauntless. She and Tris first meet when Tori is assigned to administer Tris's aptitude test, during which she warns Tris of her test's "inconclusive" result and the dangers of being Divergent. The tattoo parlor where Tori works becomes a haven for Tris during initiation, where shared confidences and bits of advice are regularly dispensed along with tea and tattoos.

ERIC

Faction: Dauntless

Dauntless Faction Leader-in-Training

"WATCH YOURSELF. WE TRAIN SOLDIERS, NOT REBELS."

Dauntless initiate instructor Eric is ruthless: Cruel and intolerant, he takes pleasure in mocking and intimidating his charges. He believes that bravery means defeating everyone, and is uninterested in recognizing or learning from the strengths of others. Eric was raised in Erudite; he and Four were Dauntless initiates together, and Eric was always ranked second, behind Four. They have been rivals ever since.

MAX

Faction: Dauntless

Dauntless Faction Leader

*"DAUNTLESS IS ABOUT
ORDINARY ACTS OF
BRAVERY AND HAVING
THE COURAGE TO STAND
UP FOR ANOTHER....
DO US PROUD."*

Under Max's leadership, the definition of Dauntless bravery is slowly shifting away from inner courage and fearlessness toward a focus on external competition and brutality. Max actually hoped to recruit Four for Eric's role as leader-in-training, but Four refused to be appointed to a position of power under Max and his vision of bravery. Relations between Max and Four have been

THE *CHOICE*

T he day before the Choosing Ceremony, those students eligible for Choosing take their aptitude test. The test is given at the city's only school, which is attended by young people from every faction.

The aptitude test is administered in a sterile classroom with a reclining chair for the student, and a computer that allows the test administrator to monitor and record results. Students may not be tested by a member of their own faction, so adults from a different faction administer the test.

The test begins with a serum that engages the mind in a series of intense simulations. These simulations feel real and produce results that the administrator can monitor on their computer screen. The simulation scenarios offer a series of high-pressure choices that measure a student's aptitude for each of the five factions. The test ends when the results leave only a single result, or aptitude, for a particular faction.

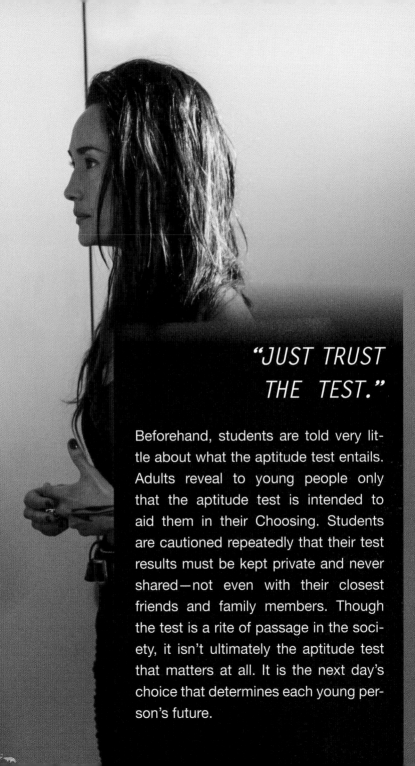

"JUST TRUST THE TEST."

Beforehand, students are told very little about what the aptitude test entails. Adults reveal to young people only that the aptitude test is intended to aid them in their Choosing. Students are cautioned repeatedly that their test results must be kept private and never shared—not even with their closest friends and family members. Though the test is a rite of passage in the society, it isn't ultimately the aptitude test that matters at all. It is the next day's choice that determines each young person's future.

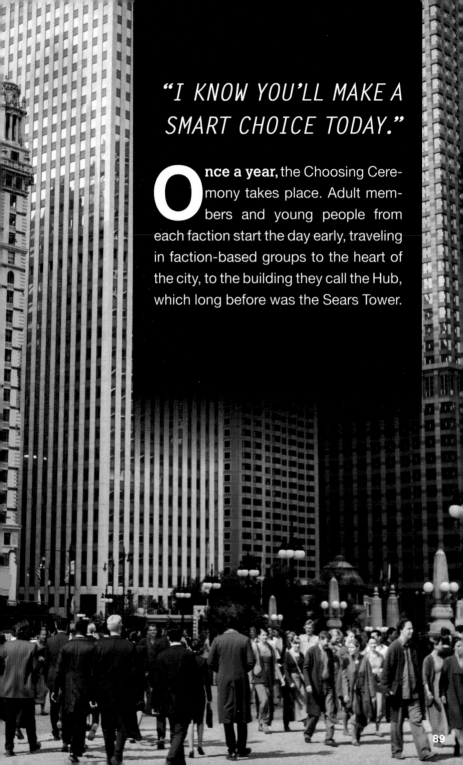

"I KNOW YOU'LL MAKE A SMART CHOICE TODAY."

Once a year, the Choosing Ceremony takes place. Adult members and young people from each faction start the day early, traveling in faction-based groups to the heart of the city, to the building they call the Hub, which long before was the Sears Tower.

89

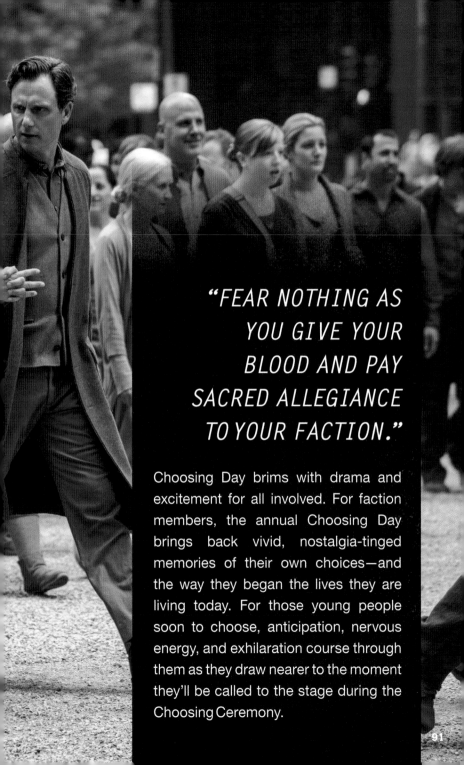

> *"FEAR NOTHING AS YOU GIVE YOUR BLOOD AND PAY SACRED ALLEGIANCE TO YOUR FACTION."*

Choosing Day brims with drama and excitement for all involved. For faction members, the annual Choosing Day brings back vivid, nostalgia-tinged memories of their own choices—and the way they began the lives they are living today. For those young people soon to choose, anticipation, nervous energy, and exhilaration course through them as they draw nearer to the moment they'll be called to the stage during the Choosing Ceremony.

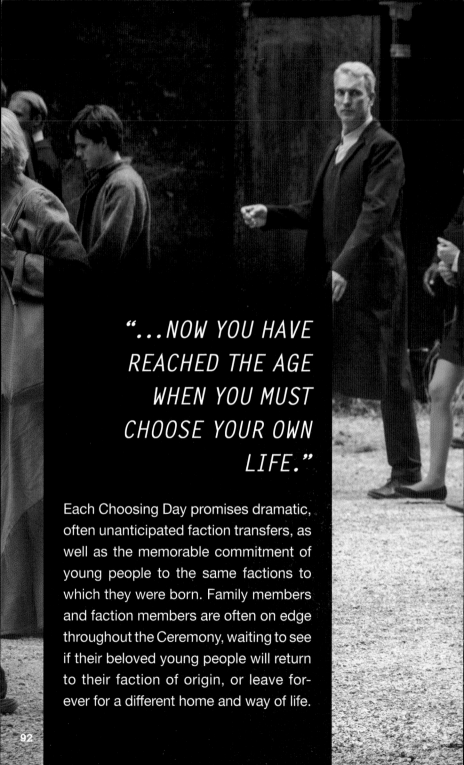

"...NOW YOU HAVE REACHED THE AGE WHEN YOU MUST CHOOSE YOUR OWN LIFE."

Each Choosing Day promises dramatic, often unanticipated faction transfers, as well as the memorable commitment of young people to the same factions to which they were born. Family members and faction members are often on edge throughout the Ceremony, waiting to see if their beloved young people will return to their faction of origin, or leave forever for a different home and way of life.

"FACTION BEFORE BLOOD"

"WHEN WE LEAVE THIS ROOM, YOU WILL NO LONGER BE DEPENDENTS BUT FULL-FLEDGED MEMBERS OF OUR SOCIETY, THE HEALTH AND SUCCESS OF WHICH NOW RESTS IN YOUR HANDS."

While the factions are devoted to their chosen virtues, one phrase holds a shared importance in all factions: the maxim "faction before blood." This statement expresses a core belief upheld by all five factions, that once chosen, the faction becomes one's most important social unit—ahead of family, friendship, mentorship, or any other aspect of social structure.

The phrase is often invoked by government officials, by faction leaders, by faction members, even by parents to their children. It can be used with equal effect as a rationale for particular behaviors, as a reminder of the proper order of things, as a motto, or as a caution.

THE CHOOSING
CEREMONY

The Choosing Ceremony begins as various faction leaders recount the history of their society, reminding those gathered of the intentions of their long-ago leaders: that faction-based, virtue-centric living would prevent conflict and lead to lasting peace. At the end of the speeches, the entire gathered assembly murmurs the motto of their society, "Faction before blood," and then a hush falls over the enormous room as the Choosing begins.

On the stage are five large bowls. Each is marked on the outside with a faction symbol and holds that faction's Choosing Ceremony substance. As each young person is called to the stage, he or she is given a knife and must cut his or her palm, spilling drops of blood into the bowl that represents his or her choice. No words are spoken by the young person; their very blood speaks for them.

The **ABNEGATION bowl** holds gray stones, the same stones used to build roads and buildings within the city. Abnegation believes stone is the most useful and stable material available, qualities they also admire as being closely related to selflessness.

The CANDOR bowl holds glass. The Candor claim that a transparent person is an honest person. They believe that glass is a visible representation of the sometimes sharp-edged transparency that their faction demands.

The **ERUDITE** **bowl** holds water. Water's clarity mirrors the clarity that Erudite members seek as they work to continually increase their knowledge. The water sends a message to would-be faction members: A single idea or simple action carries enormous weight and impact.

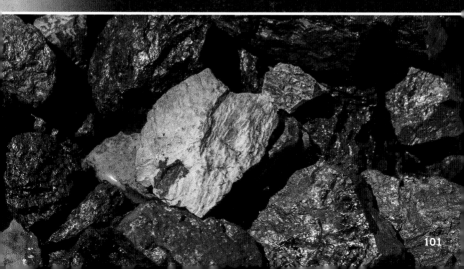

"HOWEVER, ONCE THE CHOICE HAS BEEN MADE, NO CHANGE WILL BE PERMITTED."

After the young person makes his or her choice, he or she leaves the stage and joins the chosen faction. And while it is a rule of this society's way of living that young people must be freely allowed to choose their faction, that rule does not prevent those they leave behind from feeling betrayed. Expressions of shock or relief from those gathered, from low murmurs to outright cheers, often surround a candidate as he or she joins their faction's seating area. For faction transfers, there is no moment to return to their faction of origin to bid good-bye or offer apologies or explanations—each faction exits as a whole at the Ceremony's end, and so the new lives of every young person, whether transferred or merely renewed, begin definitively and completely at the moment of choice.

ECOMING DAUNTLESS

"IS IT JUST ME OR ARE THEY TRYING TO KILL US?"

The El trains that circle the city never seem to stop, and the Dauntless are the only faction members who ride inside the train cars. When the train reaches their planned destination, the Dauntless pull open the train doors and leap out—without waiting for the train to slow down even a little, and without knowing if there's a train stop at the location or not (there's usually not).

Getting onto a train requires special courage, too. The Dauntless shun the stairs that lead to train stations, most of which are decrepit anyway, and instead scale walls and pillars, or climb whatever other architecture is necessary to arrive at the train tracks. When a train approaches, the Dauntless run alongside until their speed and momentum match that of the train. Then they leap, scramble, and lunge for handrails on the outside of the train cars. After clinging to the outside of the cars until they've caught their balance, they heave themselves through the closest doorway and into a train car. The Dauntless jump trains daily, without even seeming to consider the risk, or their own fear.

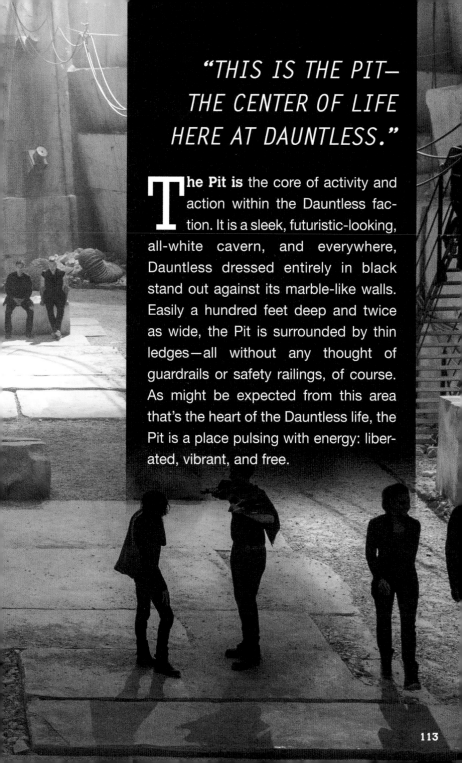

"THIS IS THE PIT— THE CENTER OF LIFE HERE AT DAUNTLESS."

The Pit is the core of activity and action within the Dauntless faction. It is a sleek, futuristic-looking, all-white cavern, and everywhere, Dauntless dressed entirely in black stand out against its marble-like walls. Easily a hundred feet deep and twice as wide, the Pit is surrounded by thin ledges—all without any thought of guardrails or safety railings, of course. As might be expected from this area that's the heart of the Dauntless life, the Pit is a place pulsing with energy: liberated, vibrant, and free.

THE CHASM

"THIS IS THE CHASM. EVERY YEAR SOMEBODY TRIES TO JUMP IT. ONE OF THEM EVEN SURVIVED. RECKLESSNESS... BRAVERY. LEARN THE DIFFERENCE."

A **narrow crevice** cuts even deeper into the rock in this portion of the Pit. A swaying, rusted bridge runs alongside it. At first glance, it seems as though one could perhaps jump across the chasm, but it's deceptively narrow, and the water that fills it is likewise deceptively shallow.

THE DAUNTLESS
UNIFORM

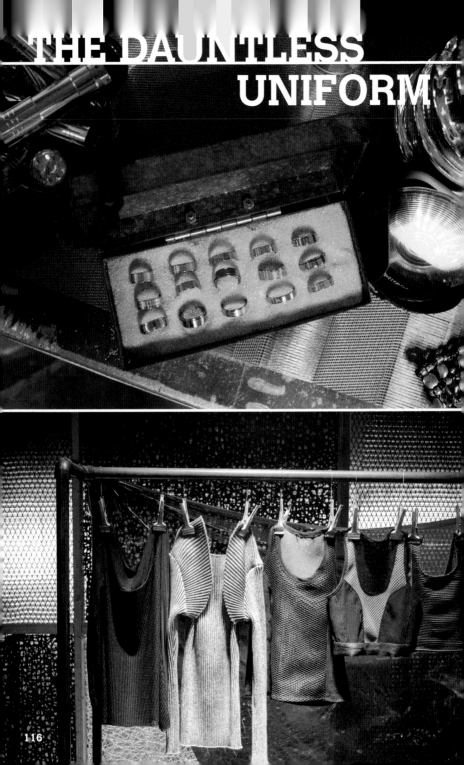

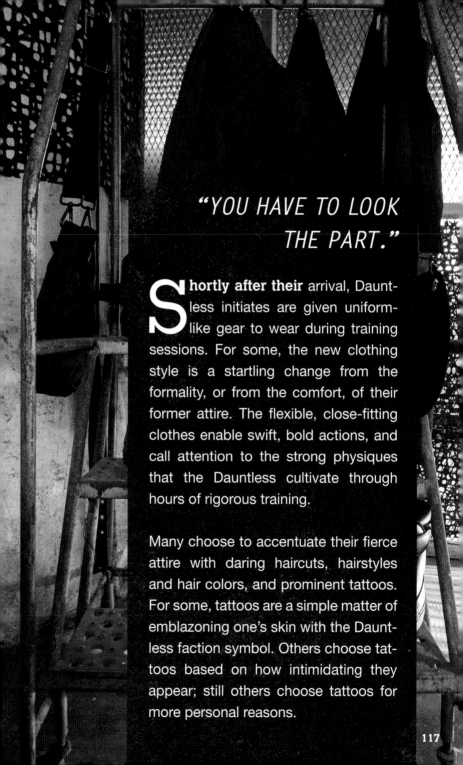

"YOU HAVE TO LOOK THE PART."

Shortly after their arrival, Dauntless initiates are given uniform-like gear to wear during training sessions. For some, the new clothing style is a startling change from the formality, or from the comfort, of their former attire. The flexible, close-fitting clothes enable swift, bold actions, and call attention to the strong physiques that the Dauntless cultivate through hours of rigorous training.

Many choose to accentuate their fierce attire with daring haircuts, hairstyles and hair colors, and prominent tattoos. For some, tattoos are a simple matter of emblazoning one's skin with the Dauntless faction symbol. Others choose tattoos based on how intimidating they appear; still others choose tattoos for more personal reasons.

THE TATTOO PARLOR

"DAUNTLESS GET TATTOOS."

The **Dauntless get** tattoos proudly and often—wearing ink on their skin is an outward sign of their willingness to undergo pain. It's also a vivid statement about the faction they belong to—no one would mistake a tattooed member of Dauntless as belonging to one of the other factions.

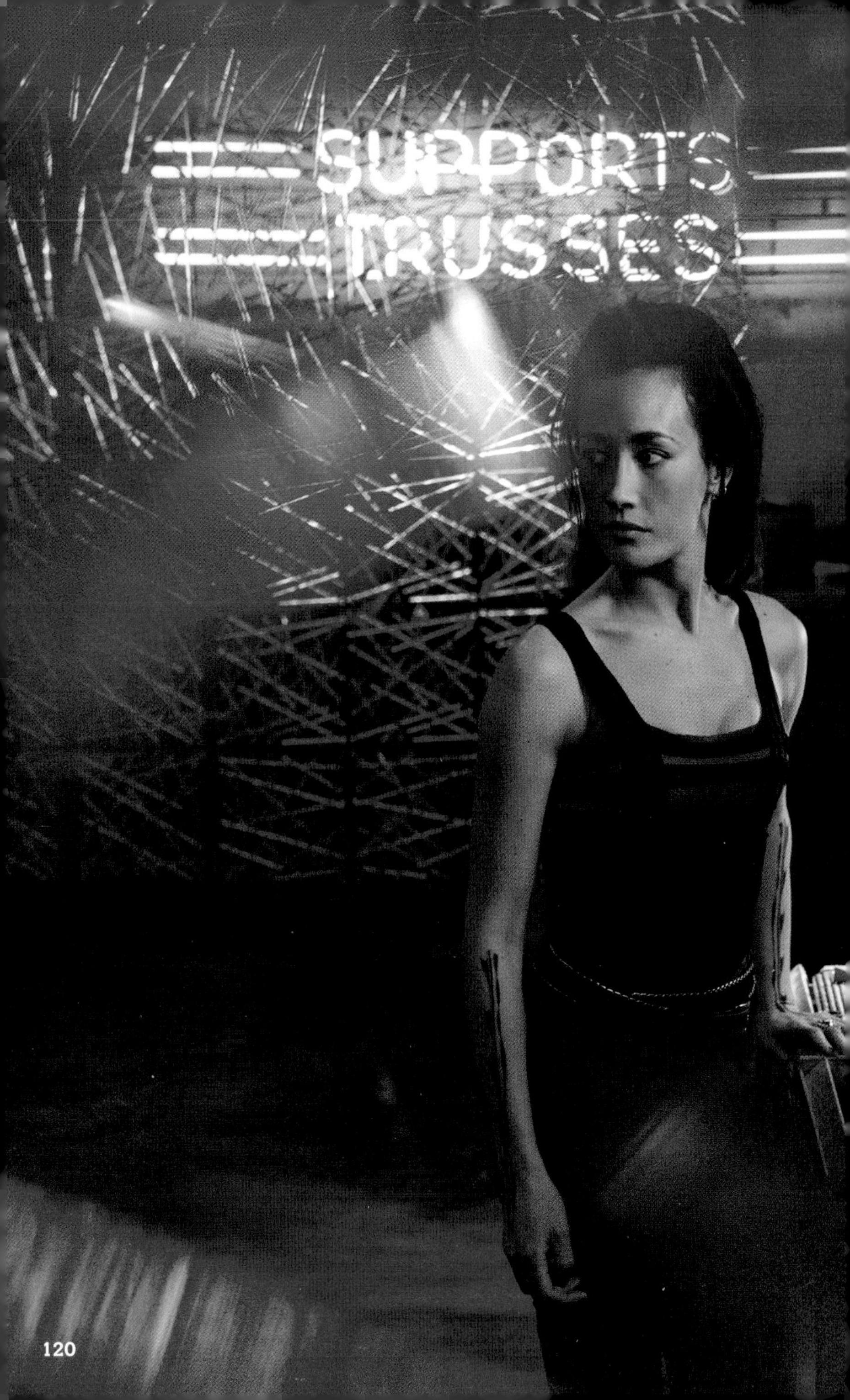
SUPPORTS
TRUSSES

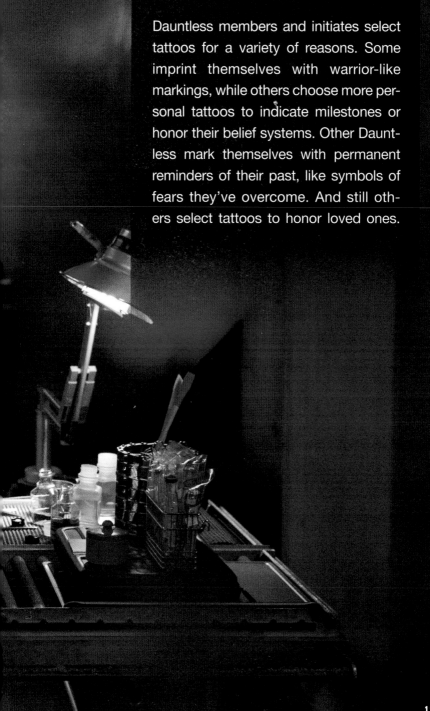

Dauntless members and initiates select tattoos for a variety of reasons. Some imprint themselves with warrior-like markings, while others choose more personal tattoos to indicate milestones or honor their belief systems. Other Dauntless mark themselves with permanent reminders of their past, like symbols of fears they've overcome. And still others select tattoos to honor loved ones.

THE DORMS

Inside the Pit, the initiates learn that they will live together for the entirety of their training/initiation period. The dorms are coed, as are the adjacent bathrooms. Both dorms and bathrooms are spartan at best: There are no walls or partitions to offer privacy, and no allowance for inhibitions.

The dorms become a hub of initiate life and emotion—for better and for worse. Alliances and friendships are formed in the dorms during downtime, but it's also a place where treacheries and betrayals happen during vulnerable, unsuspecting moments, as the initiates seek to prove their strength to one another and to the Dauntless instructors and leaders.

"IF YOU LIKE THIS, YOU'RE GONNA LOVE THE BATHROOM."

THE DINING HALL

"NICE TO MEET YOU TOO."

The **Dauntless faction** shares meals together in the cavernous dining hall, blending its members together in a sea of all-black clothing, occasionally punctuated by a shocking color of hair dye or a particularly vivid tattoo. Dauntless meals are loud, enthusiastic, and without formalities—a chaotic warmth pulses through mealtimes there, as it does through much of Dauntless life.

The Dauntless dining hall is also a central place for faction leaders to address the community, for daily faction-wide announcements to be made, and for celebrations to be hosted.

TRAINING

"THE FIRST STAGE OF TRAINING IS PHYSICAL."

Many of the days and weeks during Dauntless training will be devoted to a single thing: fighting. Dauntless instructors, Eric and Four, lead the initiates in learning sparring techniques and various methods of hand-to-hand combat. The initiates begin their work with punching bags, throwing kicks and punches alike. But this is no abstract training session. As soon as the lessons end, the practical experience begins, and the initiates are quickly set against one another in two-person skirmishes that will only end when one initiate gives up—or is knocked out cold.

"IF I SEE YOU FLINCH... YOU'RE OUT."

Dauntless training is a lot like boot camp. It begins early each morning, often with a run through the city, or with other physical warm-up exercises. One-on-one combat and sparring techniques are the foremost part of the first round of training.

Some of the initiates have never come close to a gun before, or ever used a knife for anything other than cooking. But by the time initiation ends, each initiate must be able to throw a knife with deadly accuracy, and load and fire guns without flinching—or missing a target. Training builds strength and sharpens courage in the initiates—but it also highlights their every remaining weakness.

THE RANKINGS

"YOU CHOSE US. NOW WE HAVE TO CHOOSE YOU."

Every day, the transfer initiates (and the Dauntless-born initiates) must compete against one another, and against themselves—reaching for increased levels of physical ability and decreasing their personal levels of fear.

Each evening, the Dauntless instructors rank the initiates using an electronic board. Those whose names fall "in the red" are at risk of being cut at the end of each round of training. While their eventual rankings will also be used to determine the jobs they'll take as full faction members, the primary intention of the rankings is much more immediate.

THE INFIRMARY

One place every Dauntless hopes to avoid is the infirmary. But given their tremendously aggressive lifestyle, it's not uncommon for members to find themselves in the infirmary. Dauntless hate visiting the infirmary—it wounds their pride, often to a degree that seems to nearly match the wounds on their bodies!

But when something is seriously wrong, they know there is no other choice but to seek concentrated healing. They know that their lifestyle demands a high level of physical prowess, and they are aware that losing their physical ability because of an untreated wound or a poorly healed injury would make it impossible to continue living and competing in their faction.

THE FENCE

"WE'VE SWORN AN OATH TO PROTECT EVERY LIFE INSIDE THE FENCE— WITHOUT FAIL. THAT'S WHY WE TRAIN THE WAY WE DO."

The giant fence that surrounds the city is something that members of every faction take for granted. It has been there since any of them can remember, separating the city from the marshland of what was once Lake Michigan, as well as everything beyond it.

Generations of children in the city have been taught that the fence is there to guard them, and that the Dauntless guards are there, in turn, to protect it—but that's where the certainty about the fence ends. Do even the Dauntless who guard the fence know what lies past it?

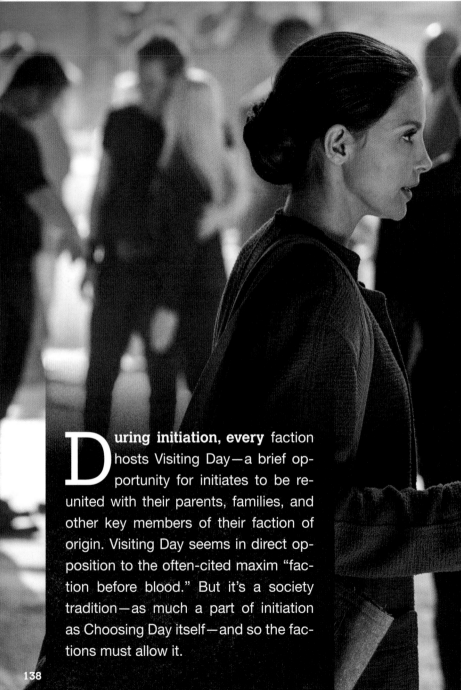

VISITING DAY

During initiation, **every** faction hosts Visiting Day—a brief opportunity for initiates to be reunited with their parents, families, and other key members of their faction of origin. Visiting Day seems in direct opposition to the often-cited maxim "faction before blood." But it's a society tradition—as much a part of initiation as Choosing Day itself—and so the factions must allow it.

In Dauntless, Visiting Day is seen as one more test—do initiates have the strength to resist being thrown off their game by reminders of old attachments? Will it be the impetus for failing initiates to quit initiation and leave altogether? Perhaps being factionless would be better than Dauntless initiation?

THE FEAR
LANDSCAPES

"THERE IS NO WAY OUT,
NO WAY OF ESCAPING
WHO YOU ARE."

The fear simulation is similar to the aptitude test, but this time instead of the serum being consumed, it will be injected—and induce hallucinations.

The serum also contains transmitters that allow instructors to see the images in the initiate's mind on a computer screen. One by one, the hallucinations take the form of the initiate's worst fears. The simulation won't be over until the initiate has faced each of his or her fears and attempted to overcome every one.

"WHAT MAKES YOU DIFFERENT MAKES YOU DANGEROUS."

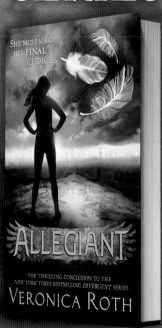

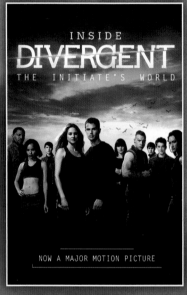